THE FIFTH OF FEBRUARY

CW00338557

Henry Normal

INTRODUCTION

This is the fifth in a series of books.

ADDITIONS TO THE FIRST EDITION

The breath within the balloon
The stain
Short trousers
Cornerhouse
Tracing the tail lights of the famous
Heavy goods vehicle
The birth of Venus
Best Room
Homing Pigeons
The Drinkers Prayer
Bus Poems
The Gallery of Harrassment
Oh to be a starling . . .
Criminal vearse
Poinst of view
The relativety of fellow travellers
To bring the word fuck into polite usage
Dancing with the truth
Concerning loss and theft
Stingray (real not marionette)
Silence of the phone

DELETIONS

Archipelagogo
There is a postcard I have never sent
The desperate vanity of change
Almost 2000 years

ALTERED

Why you never look like Paul Newman on family photos
Some kiss with their eyes closed
All matter evolves from silly string

DEDICATED TO FRANK SKINNER

All poems by HENRY NORMAL.

Cover design by EMMA DAMON.

PUBLISHED BY: A. K. PRESS
                     22 LUTTON PLACE
                     EDINBURGH
                     EH8 9PE

PRINTED IN GREAT BRITAIN BY UNICORN PRESS, SHEFFIELD.

CONTENTS

THE FIFTEENTH
OF
FEBRUARY

THE BREATH WITHIN THE BALLOON

The breath within the balloon
Will not last
You never get inflated balloons
On the Antiques Road Show
Breath brings with it vulnerability

If never inflated
A balloon may last forever
But such limp reason
Will never enchant a child
                 With decoration
Or gladden the heart
With the stretching of possibility
And the fulfilment of promise

Is not a universe of such balloons sadder
Than a universe where balloons are apt to burst

I hold your breath within my hands

The breath within the balloon will not last
But the giving of breath
And the tying of the knot
At each new birth
Is an offering
For our choice of worlds

TRAFFIC ALWAYS FLOWS FASTER THAN THE LANE TO WHICH YOU'VE SWITCHED

Giving chase
Of the ruby necklace
Heaven displays its face
Hell left within its trace

Souls returning
With diamonds burning

Ignoring the change of seasons. Without effort
The dark narrows at speed
The chain closes for comfort
Duel halos lengthen on the windscreen

A siphon to perception: Like man made couples
Two thousand tiny twilights with their own troubles

As the world and his wife with immortal flattery
Hang on the flicker of another's battery

FALLACY OF THE LOWER MIDDLE CLASS

And on the 8th day, God created the lower middle class and he spoke saying take from these terraced slums my working class people that they may settle in the new promised land we shall call council estates and give unto them extended credit facilities with no deposit and whole manner of consumer goods. Let them purchase Venetian blinds, electric door bells which play ten much loved tunes and go forth to Spain for their holiday of a lifetime bringing back a 3ft donkey and some genuine reproduction maracas.

Let them install fitted carpets, central heating and Japanese hi-fi systems into their abode. Surround them with images of style and culture that they may dwell in their illusion.

And unto them furnish sons and daughters that they may grow strong in their pretensions and flee from these places called council estates saying – 'Get behind me thee social stigma'.

And let these sons and daughters visit tasteful restaurants for evening meals and let them buy basket work and matching pine from arty shops that charge outrageous prices. And let these sons and daughters read the Daily Mail and go out in foursomes to the local lounge and talk about loft insulation, patio doors and stone fireplaces. And never, never, call these people working class for these are to be termed the lower middle class for verily the term working class is to be cast from this land for ever and ever. Amen.

WHY YOU NEVER LOOK LIKE PAUL NEWMAN
ON FAMILY PHOTOS

Snapshots snag real life
Full of misdirected angles
Blurred vision
Faces disappearing off edges
People betrayed by their expression
Likeness's half caught
Shadows masking the image
Outlines cluttered and confused
Poses thrown by the unexpected
Objects obstructing the foreground
Strangers intruding into the background
Characters unready or self conscious
Identities distorted by perspective
Detail erased by exposure
Features too close to register but more often too far away
Figures dwarfed by a vast expanse of sky

THE DREAM TICKET

. . . Man with obvious disability in maintaining relationships seeks all consuming passion but will settle for friendship and the occasional shag. Doesn't believe relationships ever work but has been known to fake undue optimism.

Woman must be classic beauty, half saint half whore (ONO). Must be 100 per cent loyal but tolerant of bumbling indiscretion. Must have no friends that she wouldn't ditch just to spend a few extra seconds in my presence. Romantic but practical. Have good sense of humour but still laugh at my weak puns.

Must be available to lavish attention on me whenever I need pampering but have interesting things to do when I'm busy so that I can be entertained when we next meet.

Must have no friends that are male, unless they are grossly ugly. All female friends should be incredibly horny and desperate to sleep with me given the slightest chance.

Must be caring and gentle in bed but willing to be ravished, tied up and have various substances smeared over specified portions of the anatomy. Must come very loudly every time we have sex. Must synchronise with each of my orgasms. Must groan and moan softly until the final stages then shout such comments as 'I've never had it so good', 'You're so big' and 'God, I love you'.

Must burst into tears for no reason occasionally and when challenged say, 'I don't want to lose you'.

Must hate everyone of my male friends. Find them sexually repulsive and inferior to me in every way. Must understand that my female friends are just friends and that's different.

Must always have a worse time than me at parties. Must hate parties, students, arty wankers, wanky art students, parties with wanky art students.

Must be completely naive, innocent and optimistic but world wise. Must be young at heart but sensible. Must be practically a virgin but have a sophisticated knowledge of sexual technique.

Must be intelligent but not so that it makes me realise my simplistic thought processes.

Most importantly must realise that all the above is not a joke.

Sent tasteful nude photo, to some anonymous box number.

STAIN

They've tried flushing

they've tried bleach

but it won't shift

they've tried scrubbing
with the little plastic brush
that matches the bath

they've even been reduced to
scouring on hands and knees
cursing their misfortune

It is never mentioned in conversation

It is ever between them

it is a guilt they share

they would move house
but for the prying of surveyors

they are looking for someone to blame

they are waiting for the other to depart

they leave the lid down
and feint problems with the plumbing
should people visit

SOME KISS WITH THEIR EYES CLOSED

Is attraction looks or deeds?
Is it one or both the heart needs?
Mannerisms enhance
The snare of romance
A virtuous act
May reinforce a lovers pact
But can deeds alone
Procure a love full grown?

From Cyrano de Bergerac
To Notre Dame's Hunchback
Though deformed
Souls perhaps better informed
To physical beauty they were drawn
A folly, a garnish, a favour worn
Needing no virtuous skill
No inner resource or act of will

Mirrored in countless books
The conclusion to which this leads
Is we judge others by their looks
But would have ourselves judged by our deeds

DEAR JOHN – THE FAX

She always put her career first
I guess I should have had a hunch
When at the moment of orgasm once
She called out 'let's do lunch'.

HEART ON A STRING

You play me like a YoYo
Taking me high
The sending me solo

JOY v ORDER

Pure loving
is
All or Nothing

Like the queue for the chippy
Outside the ground at Man City

THIRTY PEE THAT SHOOK THE WORLD

It was Chris Coupe's last thirty pee, two ten pees, a five pee, two two pees and a one. He could afford all manner of chocolate diversion but he never liked to break a thirty pee. He felt like the man in the film 'The million pound note', except not quite so rich.

Could he last the whole day on thirty pee, could he last past dinnertime. At least whilst he retained his options he was a genuine citizen, a potential consumer, an accepted member of society. The government had been farsighted enough to leave him the incentive of freedom of choice.

All the slogans and cliches he'd seen throughout his life passed in front of him: from small corns, money breeds money, speculate to accumulate, many a mickle macs a muckle. He never understood that last one.

But one thing he knew, thirty pee was hope. He was still in the game. This could be the thirty pee that shook the world. He was the thirty pee, the thirty pee was him, and he was proud of it. In his hunger he was proud. Cold and tired he was proud. He was no longer fighting for himself, he was responsible. He was struggling to keep alive the thirty pee. It was above the pettiness of self, comfort, ambition. This was a crusade for an idea. It was true freedom, true democracy, human rights, everything clean and honest worth defending.

Spend that thirty pee? No way.

Within the month Chris died, fist clenched in defiance around thirty pee, two ten pees, a five pee, two two pees, and a one.

SILENCE OF THE PHONE

The silence of the phone
Is not just the silence of one person
But the silence of all humanity

Not only does she not want to speak to you
Nobody wants to speak to you
Not one person in the entire world
You are not only alone
But snubbed, ignored
Rebuked by a conspired silence
A deliberate, vindictive silence
Not a pause or a shared silence
But a cold deslolate silence
A silence for which you are responsible
Your silence

Silences are never the same
There are many silences
The silence that passes between lovers unnoticed
The silence of a baby's sleep
The silence of
A couple trapped in each other indifference
The silence of an empty chair
The silence before a suicide
And
The silence
Of the phone is
The sum of all these
And more

CONCERNING THE LOSS AND THEFT

I've lost something valuable
or had it stolen
So I'm forced
to retrace my mundane actions
tiny harbingers who's whispers now mock with megaphones

Cursing fate and all subconscious laxity
(a betrayal that would shame Mr and Mrs Macbeth)

   The lumps on my head
from its banging against the brick wall
tell me no more than
the entrails of self loathing

   The bruising from kicking myself
promises constant dejava
a reocurring nightmare
needling
from the first to the last straw
in the proverbial hay stack

   The margin of error
I've recently allowed myself
widens from
the gap at back of a settee
to the grande canyon

Re-assessing even the most casual of contact
mistrust embitters charity
I've become Machiavelli
dusting for prints
undermining all integrity
in trial by memory

No matter whether
it turns up or not
  feel
 've lost something valuable
or had it stolen

HEAVY GOODS VEHICLE

hugging
the
inside
lane

a giant
morse
code

HGV's
own
the
dark
road
home

stamina
not
speed
now a
virtue

a slow
cure
along
the
back
bone

sleep
walking
beyond
the
cathode

pilgrims
and
heroes

A PHOTO OF THE UNIVERSE FROM THE OUTSIDE

NOW smarts like laughter in the art gallery
Like the piercing of a balloon
Abrupt to the pace of grandeur
A revelation too commonplace
Any bride and father
Awaiting the wedding car could explain

The Past – Some other lifetime away
Grows on the back of NOW
Paling intuition
A million NOW a second

The Future – A scaffold to infinity
Possible NOW to be relished
Promises of NOW in which to excel

A conscious NOW holds my hand
Deliberate amid a most solid universe.

Now so loud Cupid would need ear-muffs

THE TOURIST AND THE ANT

His speed betrays his size
His change of direction's erratic
The promise of what prize
Inspires him from the static?

Happening on a small particle
A crumb of sudden interest
Its discovery purely accidental
Is this why he forego's rest?

With the find twice his weight
And the relative distance of the patio
What instigates the social trait
That he should try to drag this home?

Is it virtue, noble and pure
Or an instinctive thought process
A malaise to which he knows no cure
Making his charity less?

Does the value of a man's deeds increase
In proportion to his intellect
Would any God of love and peace
Deny heaven to an insect?

SHORT TROUSERS

Shorts are not like short trousers

Short trousers
were just like long trousers
but shorter

to allow for scabs on your knees

Grey ones lined
with deep pockets
for keeping conkers
and galley's and bubble gum cards
and boiled sweets
with bits of fluff stuck to them

Shorts are not as substantial
flimsy approximations
worn only for set escapes
when there's an excuse
like sport
or on holiday
or occasionally
round the house
if summer stays the whole weekend
like summers when we were kids

I remember my first pair of long trousers
they made the scabs on my knees disappear
and my legs instantly grew longer
as tall as a grown up
like a detective
or a secret agent

ODE TO A STARLING
(WITH A CENTRAL MANCHESTER ADDRESS)

Perched on a ledge at Marks and Spencer
Happy to splatter all those that enter
Happy to ditch
On the heads of the rich
Or go for a shit on the Arndale Centre

DID FRANCIS OF ASSISSI HAVE THE SAME
RAPPORT WITH INSECTS?

He was the patron saint of animals
But what of the lowly insect
Would a saint covered in cockroaches
Be given the same respect?

THOUGHTS ON TAKE OFF FROM MANCHESTER AIRPORT

Must we arrive at heaven's door
Via the Wythenshawe streets
Some strange celestial package tour
All sucking boiled sweets.

STINGRAY (REAL NOT MARIONETTE)

As small hands ride these animated surfboards
rising from the water like toast from a toaster
I am unable to reach out
conscious of another injustice

the sea weed reminds me of mistletoe
and a school disco

I have felt this hestitation before

how could I kiss those lips
still bruised from another's trespass

there are some things you know without
being taught

even as she leant in for their touch

I was in love with her
and this, to me, was not about love
but a ritual mocking the appearance

there's plenty more fish in the sea
I've heard said enough times in
the twenty years since to
reinforce a place
amongst the great cliches of life

these flattened dolphins
Star Trek pancakes
charm with their trust and quirky grace

and I
have learnt to recognise
some fish affect you more than others
as do some injustices

THE BIRTH OF VENUS

Born fully grown
apart from the organics of the mundane
without the pain of stained covers
without the strains and cries of a mother

Fully grown and yet
without the realities of survival
without savage awareness
without excuses or regret

in the craft of the artist
in the dreams of romantics
in the wide eyes of lovers
she is still a child
innocent
newly born
untouched
although her nature
in melancholy is already
detached

YOU NEVER SEE A BRIGHT YELLOW HEARSE

The English don't die they just become discreet
You never see a hearse clamped on Harley Street
Or parked at a picnic site
Near lovers leap

You never see a hearse outside a betting shop
Left next to a row of prams
You never see the route to the cemetery
Served by special hearse trams

You never see a hearse at a wedding
Or on adverts for banks
Or a row of hearses at a military parade
Behind a squadron of tanks

Or outside a nightclub at closing time
With racing stripes down the bonnet
Or a hearse at the Motor Show
With dead models draped upon it

You never see a double decker hearse
Or a hearse that's extra wide
Or a hearse with 4 or 5 coffins
All crammed up inside

You never see a coffin in a sidecar
For a fanatical ex-biker
Or a hearse at a transport cafe
Picking up a hitch hiker

You never see a hearse used for ram raiding
Or a hearse with fluffy dice
Or a hearse with a taxi meter
So you can keep an eye on the price

You never see a hearse at an auction
Some dealer's trying to flog
Or a hearse with a trailer
For someone who died with their dog

Each hearse is always black and clean and neat
Because the English don't die they just become discreet.

HONEYMOON ON THE MARIE CELESTE

Take care when you're in clover
Never to appear too smug
For when your cup runneth over
It's easy to be taken for a mug.

THE PROBLEM WITH METAPHOR

Would Robert the Bruce
Have bumped his head
Half pissed on Woodpecker cider

If on the wall of the cave
He'd watched instead
A daddy longlegs not a spider.

CORNERHOUSE

Permanently at a crossroads
I glory in my window seat

The goldfish outside
Don't realise the irony
Of the screenplay for
Today I am Richard Baseheart
Schools of buses
migrate towards Piccadilly Gardens
as I chart a course
for the rest of my life
People with bigger fish to fry
circle the glass
Their faces mouthing in silence

Yesterday I was mistaken for Bergman
In Panoramic Cinemascope
Austere against a backdrop of grey and white
But no . . . I was on top of a bus
front seat
bound for Skegness

Then 2000 years later that afternoon
On the bridge of the Enterprise
I was left in control of the console
the red alert button
resembling a buttered scone
Screen on
Spock dead
My ship infested with aliens
My finger poised over a protruding sultana

But today
My body feels as heavy as a shipwreck
 am safe in the deep of my third cuppa
 eriscope down
 stening for sona
 voiding the sharks and the mermaids

THE JOY OF GIVING

Penny in the slot
Another bloody request f'
Penny in the slot
Give 'em a token gesture
Put you on the spot
Feel you're being press ganged
Put you on the spot
Can't find any less than
Penny in the slot
And a free suggestion
Try selling something
That's your best plan

Penny in the slot
A guilt nerve squeezed
Penny in the slot
A conscience eased
Penny in the slot
And you walk away pleased

Penny in the slot
It doesn't matter what you put in
It's just got to make a noise
        in the bottom of the tin

Penny in the slot
You say I've got no change
Penny in the slot
Got to save face
Penny in the slot
You say 'I already gave'

BEST ROOM

Aunty put a cover over everything
kept things nice
She lived in the living room
stored jam in the larder
and kept the lounge as the best room

There was a cover on the back
and on the arms of the settee
and on the matching armchair
although no-one ever sat on either

Covers draped over every surface or every bit of wood
softened the room
like a valley of fields or a patchwork quilt
A mirror that seldom held a close reflection shone
free of fingerprints

All her favourite ornaments
she would arrange in the China cabinet
and polish once a month

Cleaning throughout the room she would remove
each cover in turn
polish underneath
and replace the cover as before

This is the only time she would
dwell at any length in the best room

When she died, I remember
The coffin lid was so highly polished
If you got close
you could see your reflection in it
As it passed through the front room for just a moment
seemed strangely odd
without any cover

LIFE BY MAIL ORDER

There's a change of style
within your magazine
you sit there by his side
a clean cut guy
at ease he smiles
lightweight suit
well groomed hair
depth in character
a good all-rounder
drinks with the boys
knows the right people
money in the bank
at ease he smiles
at ease he smiles
within your magazine

There's a change of style
within your magazine
you stand by the blind
you turn and smile
looking good
matching pine
hanging plants
home baking
home making
freezer full of food
drapes to match the sofa
credit at your fingertips
looking good
feeling good
within your magazine

EXPERIMENTS WITH WORMS

Cut them in two
Just above the thigh
And humans do not reproduce
Both halves die

Prove this yourself
Take a human from the shelf

Now here we have a vivisectionist
Some question the workings of this
So in order to dispel doubt
Earlier I cut this one's heart out

Still we're keeping it breathing
On a cigarette machine
No need to be squeamish
It's clinically clean
And the end
Will justify the means

Vivisectionists have no feelings
Spray perfume in its eyes
Sure it cries, but it never dies
Here have a try

We've got to be cruel to be kind
And we just may find
Some medical advance
And sometimes by chance
You can be cutting up a specimen
And suddenly from the mess there in
You can make a great achievement
So we're all in agreement
We can feed tubes into his brain
And record the scale of pain

As we burn acid through his face
It's for the good of the race
Let's make this world a better place.

TRACING THE TAIL LIGHTS OF THE FAMOUS

In the film of my life
I shall appear only twice

Once looking embarrassed

Once confused

THE LAST CONTEMPLATION OF JUDAS ISCARIOT

With the guilt of his betraying kiss
Imagine Judas's exasperation
That a hanged man's final fear should be
Concerned with involuntary ejaculation

As despite his noble repentance
The image history does beg
Is of a man
With Jesus's blood upon his hands
And a trickle of sperm down his leg.

THE DEPARTMENT OF LOST WISHES

'£49.90' said the man with the clipboard
'A full refund, sign here'.

'I don't understand' I said 'refund on what?'

'£49.90, that's the total as far as our records show' he explained. 'We don't go back beyond decimalisation. Wishes made before that date come under a separate department.'

'I see', I muttered, still not understanding, 'did you say wishes?'

He tapped his pencil impatiently. 'It's all fully itemised, wishing wells, fountains, even the twenty pence you once tossed into a canal pretending it to be magical, all refundable, just sign here.'

'But I had hoped some day the wishes might . . .' I began.

He took a closer look at his clipboard and shook his head.

'I wasn't really expecting', I said feeling the need for some excuse, 'I was just hoping'.

'£49.90' he offered.

'It's not the money', I said, 'I was just hoping . . . I was just'.

'Do you want the refund or not', he insisted, 'I've got many more people to see.

'I don't think I'll sign', I said.

He made a note on his clipboard and turned to go. 'Just once I'd like to get a signature', he grumbled.

ARTHUR C. CLARKE'S AMAZING WORLD OF MANCHESTER BUSES

I knew I was in trouble after
I got stuck in a queue behind Frans Kafka
He was becoming confused and depressed
Then it came as a shock to both of us
When Godot turned up on an 81 bus
Together with the crew of the Marie Celeste

GREAT BUS JOURNEYS OF THE TWENTIETH CENTURY –
THE 79 TO CRUMPSALL

11.30 the last bus home
A mobile version of Dante's inferno
Sat aside some pissed up pubescent
About to drop his first bollock
Whose acne resembled an early Jackson Pollock
A cultured crowd as 3 or 4
Had had their heads sculptured by Henry Moore

THE CHANCES OF CATCHING A BUS TO CRUMPSALL ON A SUNDAY

You've more chance crossing the Atlantic on a busted lilo

or

Shaking hands with Venus de Milo

TINNED FRUIT AND EVAPORATED MILK

So it was last Saturday tea time when I called in at my dad's.
He was sat checking his racing results. I ambled across the room and turned off the TV. 'Just a second' I said tentatively before he started to protest, 'I've got something important to tell you'.

I hesitated a moment, then bracing myself I came right out with it, 'I love you dad' I said.

'Don't be so bloody daft', he said

'It's not daft', I said 'I love you'.

'Err . . . alright put kettle on then', he said

'No, you're supposed to say – I love you too son – c'mon dad you've seen Dallas'.

'I've not got time for all this bloody nonsense, I'm off to the Legion', he said.

So I'm following him down the garden and I'm saying, 'look dad, I'm 34 now and I think it's about time it was out in the open, I love you'.

And he's trying to shh me in case the neighbours hear.

So I shout louder, 'I don't care if the whole world hears, I'm not ashamed of my feelings, I love you, you're my dad'. And I give him a big wet kiss on the forehead. 'What do you say dad, what do you say?'

'Oh Henry', he said 'Where did I go wrong?'

POINTS OF VIEW (A CUT UP)

Hats off to the BBC
Splendid, superb, a stupendous event,
beyond belief,
I was glued to my seat
Delightful, enchanting
Many thanks to all concerned
What a pleasure it is, the find of the year,
Truly wonderful, more please,
Excellent, none will surpass,
It was really lovely
I can't thank the BBC enough
Words fail me . . . Writes
Some stuck up middle class arse licking bastard from Sidcup

CRIMINAL VERSE

Life
Is like a prison
And I'll knife anyone
Who says it isn'

DO COMMODITY BROKERS KNOW COMMODITY ONCE MEANT VAGINA?

(To the Mayor and Mayoress of Bury)

(a do-gooder is what Germans call a dildo)

Victorians would request chicken limbs
Instead of chicken legs
And enquired after chicken bosoms
As opposed to chicken breasts

Once considered worse than crumpet
Was calling a woman a buttered bun
The word bumf is short for bumfodder
Once used for wiping your bum

Poppycock means soft shit
Taking the mickey means taking the piss

When you say 'hoisted by his own petard'
Do you know that you really mean
He was in fact blown up
By his own farting machine

When you ginger up a thing
Do you know that particular phrasing
Comes from what they do to stallions
To make them rise to the occasion

Avocado is Aztec for testicle
Orchid is Greek for the same
Never mind the avocados here's the Sex Pistols
Would a flower called ballock smell the same

Once considered vulgar
Was the now polite 'bidet'
Maybe Fuck
Will be polite usage one day.

WILL SCUNTHORPE EVENTUALLY HAVE TO CHANGE IT'S NAME?

(To Tory Councillor Bigg.)

Did Bele Wydecunte (1328) have kids
Did they not take the family name
Did Simon Sitbithecunte (1167)
Feel his baptism bore him shame

What of Goodwin Clawdecunte (1066)
Did no little Clawdecuntes follow him
And did John Fillecunt (1246)
Call his son Dick on a whim

What of the ancestors of Robert Clevecunt (1302)
Did they all die in battle together
Will they too be remembered at the closing of day
Or shall their name not live forever?

THE GALLERY OF HARASSMENT

Malevolent to inertia

to jar contentment
to haunt complacency
to bait resignation

to tease the tedious and the comfortable

to taunt the skeletons from the cupboard
to aggravate the thorn in the breast
to dip hands in cold blood

to tweak the upturned nose

to worry the apathetic
to trouble the indifferent
to vex the snug

to play devil to the dull
provoke and pester, nettle and grate
to unsettle, to stimulate

the Gallery of Harassment
danes against the grain
to disturb

THE KISSING OF SCAR TISSUE

Invent them
Caress them
Nurture them
Possess them
Build your life around them
Never be found without them
Problems, appreciate them
Wallow in them
Drain every last swallow from them
You may have none tomorrow and then
You will have problems.

TO BRING THE WORD FUCK INTO POLITE USAGE

I would like us to share a fuck
a gentle fuck
a calm and tender fuck
a warm and comforting fuck
a fuck for us to cherish
honourable
exquisite
true
clean
and bright
I would like to worship you
with our fuck

FOUR SIDES DO NOT A ROUND TEA BAG MAKE

Shakespeare never used a biro
Saw a nuclear silo
Or cashed a giro

William Blake
Never bought a burger and a shake
During a commercial break
Or got turned on by a Cadbury's flake

Keats
Never saw soya meats
Or fitted sheets
Or witnessed ram raiding on inner city streets.

Edgar Allan Poe
Never had a go at comedy impro
Never caught Karaoke or faxed a photo

Wordsworth
Never gigged for clean Earth
Rode the surf,
Or read in the tabloids of a test-tube birth

Lord Byron
Never heard an air raid siren
Or watched a Quick-fit fitter fit a radial tyre on

Percy Byshe Shelley
Never saw the Simpsons on satellite telly
Or ordered decaf at the local deli

Coleridge
Never hid his dope in an ozone friendly fridge
Or slept in a cardboad box under a motorway bridge

Emily Bronte never read the Bunty
Never did the lambada or heard anything funky
Never fitted electrodes to the brain of a monkey

Language is a mirror to the culture of the day
Only the heart not the law will take a word away

I don't think I will ever see
A poem written by the EEC.

THE RELATIVETY OF FELLOW TRAVELLERS

To the naked eye
orbiting the Earth
no man made lines
may be observed

save one artificial barrier
the Great Wall of China

scarring the surface
like an old war wound
a macabre reminder
of lessons unlearned

At a distance it is possible
for a fellow traveller
to blot out the whole of humanity
with one finger

yet behind this flesh and the blood within

men will fight on different sides
no further apart their entire lives

than the thickness of skin

DRINKER'S PRAYER

Harp lager
'Till half eleven
Ale heads be thy name
Thy ring pull can
Thy swill be drunk
With burps, passing wind, heaving
Give us this day our scaly breath
And forgive us our dropped glasses
As we forgive them that toss glasses against us
Lead us not to attempt Asian take-aways
But deliver us from seafood
For opening time is for drinking
'Till all hours of the morning
Forever and ever
Same again

THE DEHUMANISING OF PREY

Aside a boat about the Canaries
A fish floats around and varies
Its course to take the bait
And tourists wait
'Til Everyone's a winner
The fish placed in a
Plastic bucket
Novices can't believe their luck at
Such a sport
Struck at how much their hook has caught
They watch the catch fight and squirm
'But does the biting of the hook do harm?'
I wonder, as later on land it's
Sport for time-share bandits
To hook with lines a little shorter
Bigger fish out of water

TIME SHARE

Standing at the gates of Heaven in odd socks
Over zealous
I've wasted half my life lusting after women or being jealous

It's not the functional but ornamentation people seek out/
Admire/hold in wonderment

The eye focuses on any movement
Expectation sells
This is the age of the beggar with a moneybelt

Yet without wasps and bees
They'd be no flowers and trees

Overspill and preferred delusion
Compromise is coming to terms with losing

You are the victim of my circumstance
As I am the victim of yours
With your legs about my naked back
Nature holds no greater rapport

Deliver us from the rhetoric of passion
Bathe your feet in the deep
And cover me with your lashes.

OSTRICH MAN

I can see no evil in the world
There's nothing can make me sad
I can't see anything because
My head's inside this bag

I'm not an animal, I'm a man
I was given this by my dad
He said one day everything you see will be yours
Then he gave me this bloody bag

The teachers gave me another
I got a further one from my mother
They gave me one at every job I had
They said 'we can see a great future for you son
Here wear this very nice bag'

But now I'm dead they say I can take it off
But though they think I'm mad
I'll show them they can't discipline me
See, I'm still wearing my bag

I showed them didn't I? I showed them.

ATTACK OF THE FIFTY FOOT EGO

David Lawson's ego had grown enormously since he saw his work in print. He paraded his ego daily, took it for long walks. Sat it on his knee in the pub. It became his only topic of conversation.

At night he began to feed it with the odd passing acquaintance and very soon it developed a liking for flesh. It's appetite grew and not before long old friends, distant relations and gradually complete strangers were ferociously attacked and left for dead.

Becoming uncontrollable his ego enlarged with each victim it devoured. No longer were individuals enough, his ego began to challenge small groups, tupperware parties, crochet clubs, easy meat. Stronger and stronger it became; now Rugby clubs and Kung Fu night classes fell victim. Not only third division football teams but their supporters as well it assaulted en masse. Small northern towns it savaged without mercy. As his ego towered up to a giant fifty feet it began it's attack on London, the Queen, the Armed Forces, Parliament and the Police leaving them all devastated.

Brushing aside the Archbishop of Canterbury, The Pope and even Billy Graham the ego threw out a challenge to God himself. A fair fight the ego insisted. God remained silent. To limber up the ego ransacked America and held up the blood of Hollywood. 'Now', said the ego from the top of the Empire State building, send down the Four Horsemen of the Apocalypse and I'll tie one hand behind my back'. Nothing happened.

'OK God', threatened the ego, 'I'm coming for you', and it leapt out into that great boxing ring in the sky. Four thousand feet later garbage men scraped the remains of David Lawson off the sidewalk. 'First round to me' said God. 'Low punch', the ego protested biting hard on God's ankles.

THE MORNING AFTER PILLOW

Does love sleep?
Or keep its favour
Or cradle a nightmare of a
Different colour
Hesitating in the middle distance
Blocking the lane for the ambulance

Between the eroticism of detail
And an indefinite article

Devotion torn from the gift wrapping
Discolouring the hunger of stained glass

Like the inflatable globe that blows up in your face
Like the juggler trying to cover his fourth mistake

A blizzard of the heart
And the domino of principles

The domino of principles
And a blizzard of the heart

The 14th and 15th of February
Are only an eyelid apart.

BOOKS BY HENRY NORMAL NOW IN PRINT –

From:

A..K. DISTRIBUTION,
22 LUTTON PLACE,
EH8 9PE
TEL:/FAX: 031 6671507

A MORE INTIMATE FAME

A5 Book, 120 pages, glossy cover, bound.
Price £6.60 (inc. p&p).

THE DREAM TICKET (Second Edition)

A5 Booklet, 52 pages, glossy cover, bound.
Price £5.40 (inc. p&p).

THE FIFTEENTH OF FEBRUARY (Second Edition)

A5 Booklet, 52 pages, glossy cover, bound.
Price £5.40 (inc. p&p).

THE THIRD PERSON

A5 Booklet, 56 pages, glossy cover, bound.
Price £5.40 (inc. p&p).

Some Recent Titles from AK Press

ECSTATIC INCISIONS: THE COLLAGES OF FREDDIE BAER by Freddie Baer, preface by Peter Lamborn Wilson; ISBN 1 873176 60 0; 80 pages, a three color cover, perfect bound 8 1/2 x 11; £7.95. This is Freddie Baer's first collection of collage work; over the last decade her illustrations have appeared on numerous magazine covers, posters, t-shirts, and album sleeves. Includes collaborations with Hakim Bey, T. Fulano, Jason Keehn, and David Watson.

SOME RECENT ATTACKS: ESSAYS CULTURAL AND POLITICAL - by James Kelman; ISBN 1 873176 80 5; 96pp; £4.50. In this collection, Kelman directs his linguistic craftsmanship and scathing humor at targets ranging from "private profit and public loss" to the "endemic racism, class bias and general elitism at the English end of the Anglo-American literary tradition."

INNA LIVERPOOL - by Benjamin Zephaniah; ISBN 1 873176 75 9; 24pp; £1.95. A selection of poems representing a small portion of Zephaniah's work as Poet/Writer in Residence with the Africa Arts Collective in 1988/89.

ON THE MASS BOMBING OF IRAQ AND KUWAIT, COMMONLY KNOWN AS THE "GULF WAR" - by Tom Leonard; ISBN 1 873176252; 24pp; £1.95. Written as the 'allies' perpetrated the mass execution of the Iraqi people, On the Mass Bombing ... exposes the hypocrisy and deceit of politicians and the military, and the media's complicity, in a concerted attempt at the wholesale destruction of a country, its people and infrastructure.

THE ASSAULT ON CULTURE: UTOPIAN CURRENTS FROM LETTRISME TO CLASS WAR - by Stewart Home; ISBN 1 873176 30 9; 128pp two color cover perfect bound 5 1/2 x 8 1/2; £5.95. "A straightforward account of the vanguards that followed Surrealism: Fluxus, Lettrisme, Neoism, and other even more obscure." *Village Voice.*

AK Press publishes, distributes to the trade, and retails mail order a wide variety of radical literature. For our latest catalog featuring these and several thousand other titles, please send a large self-addressed, stamped envelope to:

AK Press
22 Lutton Place
Edinburgh, Scotland
EH8 9PE, Great Britain

AK Press
P.O. Box 40682
San Francisco, CA
94140-0682 U.S.A.